TOUGH QUESTIONS
REVISED EDITION

HOW COULD GOD ALLOW SUFFERING AND EVIL?

The Tough Questions Series

TOUGH
QUESTIONS
EVISED EDITION

HOW COULD

GOD ALLOW

SUFFERING

AND EVIL?

HOW COULD
GOD ALLOW
SUFFERING
AND EVIL?

GARRY POOLE

foreword by **Lee Strobel**

WILLOW
CREEK
RESOURCES

ZONDERVAN™

GRAND RAPIDS, MICHIGAN 49530 USA

We want to hear from you. Please send your comments about this book to us in care of zreview@zondervan.com. Thank you.

ZONDERVAN™

How Could God Allow Suffering and Evil?
Copyright © 1998, 2003 by Willow Creek Association

Requests for information should be addressed to:

Zondervan, *Grand Rapids, Michigan 49530*

ISBN: 0-310-24505-2

Interior design by Nancy Wilson

Printed in the United States of America

03 04 05 06 07 08 09 /❖ CH/ 10 9 8 7 6 5 4 3 2 1

Contents

Foreword

For most of my life I was an atheist. I thought that the Bible was hopelessly riddled with mythology, that God was a man-made creation born of wishful thinking, and that the deity of Jesus was merely a product of legendary development. My no-nonsense education in journalism and law contributed to my skeptical viewpoint. In fact, just the idea of an all-powerful, all-loving, all-knowing creator of the universe seemed too absurd to even justify the time to investigate whether there could be any evidence backing it up.

However, my agnostic wife's conversion to Christianity, and the subsequent transformation of her character and values, prompted me to launch my own spiritual journey in 1980. Using the skills I developed as the legal affairs editor of *The Chicago Tribune*, I began to check out whether any concrete facts, historical data, or convincing logic supported the Christian faith. Looking back, I wish I had this curriculum to supplement my efforts.

This excellent material can help you in two ways. If you're already a Christ-follower, this series can provide answers to some of the tough questions your seeker friends are asking—or you're asking yourself. If you're not yet following Christ but consider yourself either an open-minded skeptic or a spiritual seeker, this series can also help you in your journey. You can thoroughly and responsibly explore the relevant issues while discussing the topics in community with others. In short, it's a tremendous guide for people who really want to discover the truth about God and this fascinating and challenging Nazarene carpenter named Jesus.

If the previous paragraph describes you in some way, prepare for the adventure of a lifetime. Let the pages that follow take you on a stimulating journey of discovery as you grapple with the most profound—and potentially life-changing—questions in the world.

—Lee Strobel, author of
The Case for Christ and *The Case for Faith*

Getting Started

Welcome to the Tough Questions series! This small group curriculum was produced with the conviction that claims regarding spiritual truth can and should be tested. Religions—sometimes considered exempt from scrutiny—are not free to make sweeping declarations and demands without providing solid reasons why they should be taken seriously. These teachings, including those from the Bible in particular, purport to explain the most significant of life's mysteries, with consequences alleged to be eternal. Such grand claims should be analyzed carefully. If this questioning process exposes faulty assertions, it only makes sense to refuse to place one's trust in these flawed systems of belief. If, on the other hand, an intense investigation leads to the discovery of truth, the search will have been worth it all.

Christianity contends that God welcomes sincere examination and inquiry; in fact, it's a matter of historical record that Jesus encouraged such scrutiny. The Bible is not a secret kept only for the initiated few, but an open book available for study and debate. The central teachings of Christianity are freely offered to all, to the skeptic as well as to the believer.

So here's an open invitation: explore the options, examine the claims, and draw your conclusions. And once you encounter and embrace the truth—look out! Meaningful life-change and growth will be yours to enjoy.

It is possible for any of us to believe error; it is also feasible for us to resist truth. Using this set of discussion guides will help you sort out the true from the supposed, and ultimately offer a reasonable defense of

> You will seek me and find me when you seek me with all your heart.
>
> —Jeremiah 29:13

the Christian faith. Whether you are a nonbeliever or skeptic, or someone who is already convinced and looking to fortify your faith, these guides will lead you to a fascinating exploration of vital spiritual truths.

Tough Questions for Small Groups

The Tough Questions series is specifically designed to give spiritual seekers (or non-Christians) a chance to raise questions and investigate the basics of the Christian faith within the safe context of a seeker small group. These groups typically consist of a community of two to twelve seekers and one or two leaders who gather on a regular basis, primarily to discuss spiritual matters. Seeker groups meet at a wide variety of locations, from homes and offices to restaurants and churches to bookstores and park district picnic tables. A trained Christian leader normally organizes the group and facilitates the discussions based on the seekers' spiritual concerns and interests. Usually, at least one apprentice (or coleader) who is also a Christian assists the group leader. The rest of the participants are mostly, if not all, non-Christians. This curriculum is intended to enhance these seeker small group discussions and create a fresh approach to exploring the Christian faith.

Because the primary audience is the not-yet-convinced seeker, these guides are designed to represent the skeptical, along with the Christian, perspective. While the truths of the Christian position are strongly affirmed, it is anticipated that non-Christians will dive into these materials with a group of friends and discover that their questions and doubts are not only well understood and represented here, but also valued. If that goal is accomplished, open and honest discussions about Christianity can follow. The greatest hope behind the formation of this series is that seekers will be challenged in a respectful way to seriously consider and even accept the claims of Christ.

A secondary purpose behind the design of this series is to provide a tool for small groups of Christians to use as they discuss answers to the tough questions seekers are asking. The process of wrestling through these important questions and issues will not only strengthen their own personal faith, but also provide them with insights for entering into informed dialogues about Christianity with their seeking friends.

A hybrid of the two options mentioned above may make more sense for some groups. For example, a small group of Christians may want to open up their discussion to include those who are just beginning to investigate spiritual things. This third approach provides an excellent opportunity for both Christians and seekers to examine the claims of Christianity together. Whatever the configuration of your group, may you benefit greatly as you use these guides to fully engage in lively discussions about issues that matter most.

Guide Features

The Introduction

At the beginning of every session is an introduction, usually several paragraphs long. You may want to read this beforehand even though your leader will probably ask the group to read it aloud together at the start of every meeting. These introductions are written from a skeptical point of view, so a full spectrum of perspectives is represented in each session. Hopefully, this information will help you feel represented, understood, and valued.

Open for Discussion

Most sessions contain ten to fifteen questions your group can discuss. You may find that it is difficult for your group to get through all these questions in one sitting. That is okay; the important thing is to engage in the topic at hand—not to necessarily get through every question. Your group, however, may decide to spend more than one meeting on each session in order to address all of the questions. The Open for Discussion sections are designed to draw out group participation and give everyone the opportunity to process things openly.

Usually, the first question of each session is an "icebreaker." These simple questions are designed to get the conversation going by prompting the group to discuss a nonthreatening issue, usually having to do with the session topic to be covered. Your group may want to make time for additional icebreakers at the beginning of each discussion.

Charting Your Journey

The purpose of the "Charting Your Journey" section is to challenge you to go beyond a mere intellectual and emotional discussion to personal application. This group experience is, after all, a journey, so each session includes this section devoted to helping you identify and talk about your current position. Your views will most likely fluctuate as you make new discoveries along the way.

Heart of the Matter

The section called "Heart of the Matter" represents a slight turn in the group discussion. Generally speaking, the questions in this section speak more to the emotional, rather than just the intellectual, side of the issue. This is an opportunity to get in touch with how you feel about a certain aspect of the topic being discussed and to share those feelings with the rest of the group.

Straight Talk

Every session has at least one section, called "Straight Talk," designed to stimulate further thinking and discussion around relevant supplementary information. The question immediately following Straight Talk usually refers to the material just presented, so it is important that you read and understand this part before you attempt to answer the question.

Quotes

Scattered throughout every session are various quotes, many of them from skeptical or critical points of view. These are simply intended to spark your thinking about the issue at hand.

Scripture for Further Study

This section ends each session with a list of suggested Scripture passages that relate to the discussion topic.

Recommended Resources

This section at the back of each guide lists recommended books that may serve as helpful resources for further study.

Discussion Guidelines

These guides, which consist mainly of questions to be answered in your group setting, are designed to elicit dialogue rather than short, simple answers. Strictly speaking, these guides are not Bible studies, though they regularly refer to biblical themes and passages. Instead, they are topical discussion guides, meant to get you talking about what you really think and feel. The sessions have a point and attempt to lead to some resolution, but they fall short of providing the last word on any of the questions raised. That is left for you to discover for yourself! You will be invited to bring your experience, perspective, and uncertainties to the discussion, and you will also be encouraged to compare your beliefs with what the Bible teaches in order to determine where you stand as each meeting unfolds.

Your group should have a discussion leader. This facilitator can get needed background material for each session in the *Tough Questions Leader's Guide*. There, your leader will find some brief points of clarification and understanding (along with suggested answers) for many of the questions in each session. The supplemental book *Seeker Small Groups* is also strongly recommended as a helpful resource for leaders to effectively start up small groups and facilitate discussions for spiritual seekers. *The Complete Book of Questions: 1001 Conversation Starters for Any Occasion*, a resource filled with icebreaker questions, may be a useful tool to assist everyone in your group to get to know one another better, and to more easily launch your interactions.

In addition, keep the following list of suggestions in mind as you prepare to participate in your group discussions.

1. The Tough Questions series does not necessarily need to be discussed sequentially. The guides, as well as individual sessions, can be mixed and matched in any order and easily discussed independently of each other, based on everyone's interests and questions.

2. If possible, read over the material before each meeting. Familiarity with the topic will greatly enrich the time you spend in the group discussion.

3. Be willing to join in the group interaction. The leader of the group will not present a lecture but rather will encourage each of you to openly discuss your opinions and disagreements. Plan to share your ideas honestly and forthrightly.

4. Be sensitive to the other members of your group. Listen attentively when they speak and be affirming whenever you can. This will encourage

more hesitant members of the group to participate. Always remember to show respect toward
the others even if they don't always agree with
your position.

5. Be careful not to dominate the discussion. By all
means participate, but allow others to have
equal time.

6. Try to stick to the topic being studied. There
won't be enough time to handle the peripheral
tough questions that come to mind during your
meeting.

7. It would be helpful for you to have a good mod-
ern translation of the Bible, such as the New
International Version, the New Living Translation, or the New American Standard Bible. You
might prefer to use a Bible that includes notes
especially for seekers, such as *The Journey: The
Study Bible for Spiritual Seekers*. Unless noted
otherwise, questions in this series are based on
the New International Version.

8. Do some extra reading in the Bible and other
recommended books as you work through these
sessions. To get you started, the "Scripture for
Further Study" section lists several Bible refer-
ences related to each discussion, and the "Recommended Resources" section at the back of
each guide offers some ideas of books to read.

Unspeakable Love

Christianity stands or falls on Christ. Yet he left us
with a whole lot of hard sayings. But the central scan-
dal of Christianity is that at a point in history, God
came down to live among us in a person, Jesus of
Nazareth. And the most baffling moment of Jesus' life
was on the cross, where he hung to die like a common
criminal. In that place of weakness—where all seemed
lost, where the taunts of "Prove yourself, Jesus, and

come down from there!" lashed out like the whip that flogged him prior to his crucifixion—somehow God was at his best. There at the cross, he expressed a love greater than words could ever describe. That act of Jesus, presented as the ultimate demonstration of the love and justice of God, begs to be put to "cross" examination.

As you wrestle with these tough questions, be assured that satisfying, reasonable answers are waiting to be found. And you're invited to discover them with others in your small group as you explore and discuss these guides. God bless you on your spiritual journey!

Seek and you will find; knock and the door will be opened to you.

—Matthew 7: 7

How Could God Allow Suffering and Evil?

Adolph Hitler. Tornadoes. Inoperable cancer. Car accidents. Terrorist bombings. AIDS. Drive-by shootings. Child abuse. September 11, 2001.

With just a few words, chills run down our spines and we feel sick to our stomachs. Images flash before us that generate deep emotional reactions. What stirs up all our fear, outrage, and anger? It can be summed up in one word: *evil.*

When something terrible happens to us, we grope for explanations. Why does evil torment our lives? Where does it come from? How will we ever get past it?

Some people blame nature and its randomness. Some blame a few sinister but powerful people. Some blame themselves. Some believe there is a malicious force at work, a devil or evil spirits. And each of us—at one time or another—has probably blamed God.

Where does evil come from? Isn't it reasonable—maybe even logically necessary—to ascribe it to God? He made everything; he must have also made evil. And what exactly is evil? Is it a living entity, maliciously aiming its terrifying arrows at hapless humans? Is it mere randomness—chaos masquerading as unkindness? Or maybe evil is part of God—the "Dark Side of the Force" that's as necessary as his good side.

Maybe God's testing us—he's watching to see how we'll handle all this pain and suffering. Maybe it's punishment—he's telling us, "This is what you deserve for the life you've lived!" Or maybe the universe just

> If any spirit created the universe, it is malevolent, not benevolent.
>
> —Quentin Smith,
> *The Anthropic Coincidences, Evil and the Disconfirmation of Theism*

17

got away from God, like a science experiment gone awry. He'd like to fix it, but it's just too out of control.

All these thoughts about evil can lead us to one nagging question: "Why does God allow it?" Maybe right now this is *your* big question. If it is, you're in the right place. Fully explore this issue in all its rawness, being honest with yourself and with others about the pain and confusion you feel.

Six sessions devoted to this subject will probably not answer every question and certainly won't heal every ache in your heart. But Christianity does purport to deal with this issue, and the Bible speaks to the reasons behind evil and to the way for us to cope with it. Tread carefully, but deliberately, and see for yourself if there are not answers—and encouragement—awaiting.

Where Did Evil Come From?

What's Wrong with This Picture?

Look around us. We live in a messed-up world. Disease, death, and misery envelop the planet. Strife exists between people and nations. This is a dark place to live, and while at times a ray of beauty or hope shines through, it is clouded over by the next senseless murder or "natural" disaster. Is this the world God created? Surely the perfect-world story of the Garden of Eden was a myth. This planet could never have existed in that condition. Suffering and evil are the unvarnished facts of "creation"—not that fairy tale of a paradise.

In his novel *Catch-22,* one of Joseph Heller's characters, Yossarian, holds the following conversation with Lt. Scheisskopf's wife:

> "Don't tell me God works in mysterious ways. There's nothing so mysterious about it. He's not working at all. He's playing. Or else he's forgotten all about us. . . . How much reverence can you have for a Supreme being who finds it necessary to include such phenomena as phlegm and tooth decay in his divine system of creation? What in the world was going through that warped, evil, scatological mind of his when he robbed old people of the ability to control their bowel movements? Why in the world did he ever create pain? . . . Why couldn't he have used a doorbell instead to notify us, or one of his

> If such a God did exist, he could not be a beneficent God, such as the Christians posit. What effrontery is it that talks about the mercy and goodness of a nature in which all animals devour animals, in which every mouth is a slaughter-house and every stomach a tomb!
>
> —E. M. McDonald,
> *An Anthology of Atheism and Rationalism*

celestial choirs? Or a system of red-and-blue neon tubes right in the middle of each person's forehead? . . . What a colossal, immortal blunderer! When you consider the opportunity and power he had to really do a job, and then look at the stupid, ugly little mess he made of it instead, his sheer incompetence is almost staggering. . . . Why, no self-respecting businessman would hire a bungler like him as even a shipping clerk!"

"Stop it! Stop it!" Lieutenant Scheisskopf's wife screamed suddenly. . . . "Stop it!"

"I thought you didn't believe in God," he asked bewilderedly.

"I don't," she sobbed. . . . "But the God I don't believe in is a good God, a just God, a merciful God. He's not the mean and stupid God you make him out to be."

In the face of the undeniable existence of pain and evil, who can believe in a good God behind this mess? We must conclude he's either a poor creator or a poor redeemer. He either intended this mess—a shudder goes through us at that thought—or once he made the mistake, he was too inept to make it right.

Is there any possible excuse for the way things are? If this is all from God, what explains the origin—and persistence—of that which is supposed to be antithetical to his nature?

OPEN FOR DISCUSSION

1. Describe a recent encounter you've had with some form of evil, which prompted you to wonder why this kind of thing ever happens.

2. Who or what did you blame for the wrong that occurred in the situation you described above? Give reasons for your response. How did those around you see the situation?

The Bible tells us to be like God, and then on page after page it describes God as a mass murderer. This may be the single most important key to the political behavior of Western Civilization.

—Robert A. Wilson,
*Right Where You
Are Sitting Now*

STRAIGHT TALK

Moral and Natural Evil

Philosophers have categorized two kinds of evil:

moral evil — man's own inhumanity to man, based on hate, greed, or overindulgence
natural evil — evils brought on by natural causes in the world, such as floods, earthquakes, or tornadoes and different sorts of diseases, accidents, and injuries

3. Using your previous example, would you categorize that evil you experienced as moral evil, natural evil, or a combination of the two? Why? Does the category or type of evil influence how you determine where to place the blame for evil?

The vast majority of human evil and suffering is a direct result of human irresponsibility.

—Cliffe Knechtle,
Give Me an Answer

4. Take your best shot at briefly explaining why we live in a world filled with so much evil and suffering.

STRAIGHT TALK

Unable or Unwilling?

Doesn't it make sense that God, by default, is the author of evil if he created everything else? This progression of thought usually brings people full circle, back to wondering what kind of God exists — or even if he does exist.

Echoing Epicurus, David Hume, the eighteenth-century Scottish skeptic, put it this way: "Is he willing to prevent evil, but not able? Then he is impotent. Is he able, but not willing? Then he is malevolent. Is he both able and willing? Whence then is evil?"

---

5. Summarized below are two conclusions based on the above observations. Defend or refute the logic behind each.

Because we live in a world where evil does exist,

- God must not really exist after all; otherwise he would not have created such a place filled with evil.
- God might still exist, but not in the way the Bible depicts him (as all-powerful and loving); otherwise he would have had both the ability and the desire to create a world without so much evil.

STRAIGHT TALK
The Free-Choice Risk

Here is a very different argument addressing the problem of evil.

1. God created the universe without evil and suffering.
2. God created perfect human beings.
3. God created humans with a complete ability to freely choose between staying in harmony with God or rejecting him.
4. Humankind freely chose to turn away from God.
5. Evil and suffering entered the world as a result of that separation from God.

Norman Geisler describes the above reasoning this way: "We have a real choice about what we do. God made us that way so we could be like him and could love freely (forced love is not love at all, is it?). But in making us that way, he also allowed for the possibility of evil. To be free we had to have not only the opportunity to choose good, but also the ability to choose evil. That was the risk God knowingly took. That doesn't make him responsible for evil. He created the *fact* of freedom; we perform the *acts* of freedom. He [God] made evil *possible*; men made evil *actual*."

And Cliffe Knechtle states in his book *Give Me an Answer*, "Genesis 1 clearly communicates that when God created, all his creation was very good. God did not create evil, suffering or death. He created us to enjoy himself, each other and to celebrate his gift of life. Genesis 3 is the tragic record of how man and woman chose to reject God. The Bible, history books and the morning newspaper record how an immeasurable amount of evil has followed in the wake of human rebellion against God. The vast majority of this carnage is a direct result of human choice."

6. The above explanation introduces the element of a free choice by humankind to reject or accept God—with resulting consequences. Given the magnitude of the risk, what value do

Babies are born with multiple birth defects. Genetic disorders plague many of us. An earthquake levels a city, and thousands lose their lives in the rubble. The Bible teaches that there is not always a one-to-one correspondence between sin and suffering. When we human beings told God to shove off, he partially honored our request. Nature began to revolt. The earth was cursed. Genetic breakdown and disease began. Pain and death became a part of the human experience. The Good creation was marred. We live in an unjust world. We are born into a world made chaotic and unfair by a humanity in revolt against its Creator.

—Cliffe Knechtle,
Give Me an Answer

you suppose God placed on granting people freedom of choice (according to this perspective)?

7. How would you explain the correlation between separation from God and the entrance of evil and suffering into the world?

8. Share your opinion of the following statement: "God cannot both create human beings with a total ability to freely make meaningful choices and at the same time control them so they always choose good."

HEART OF THE MATTER

9. Do you consider your freedom of choice to be a gift from God? Why or why not? What would human relationships be like without free will?

10. If you could eliminate all evil, suffering, and sin (wrongdoing) in your life by giving up your free will, would you do it? Explain.

11. Do you ever become angry at God for the things that go wrong in your life? Why or why not?

CHARTING YOUR JOURNEY

With this session you're beginning a journey. Keep in mind that you do not need to feel pressured to "say the right thing" at any point during these discussions. You're taking the time to do this work because you're looking for answers and because you're willing to be honest about your doubts and uncertainties. Others in your group would also benefit from hearing about what you'll be learning. So use these sessions profitably—ask the tough questions, think "outside the box," and learn from what others in your group have to say. But stay authentic about where you are in your journey.

To help you identify your progress more clearly, throughout this guide you will have opportunities to indicate where you are in your spiritual journey. As you gain more spiritual insights, you may find yourself reconsidering your opinions from session to session. The important thing is for you to be completely truthful about what you believe—or don't believe—right now.

12. Check the statement(s) below that best describes your position at this point. Share your selection with the rest of the group and give reasons for your response.

_____ I believe that the origin of evil is ultimately God's responsibility.

_____ I'm convinced that evil is the result of humankind's rejection of God.

_____ Evil is a misnomer; the universe operates without a moral component.

_____ I'm fairly certain that our freedom to choose is a gift from God.

_____ I'm convinced that our freedom to choose has nothing to do with God.

_____ I find myself blaming God for things that go wrong in my life.

_____ I find myself blaming myself for things that go wrong in my life.

_____ Write your own brief phrase here: _____

_____

_____

Scripture for Further Study

- Genesis 1–3
- Job 1:6–11
- Job 5:7
- Isaiah 30:18
- Luke 22:28–34
- John 9:1–3
- John 16:33

- Romans 5:3, 12–21
- Romans 12:12
- 2 Corinthians 4:16–18
- Ephesians 2:1–2
- Ephesians 6:10–19
- James 1:2–4

Why Do Innocent People Suffer?

It's Not Fair

The man in the interview struggled to stay in control. He clutched the shoulders of his wife, who grieved openly. The reporter was speaking to the couple in front of their little boy's school. Nearby lay a toppled bike. Blood covered the sidewalk.

"Two nine-year-old boys had just left school on their bikes when shots rang out from a passing car," the reporter stated, facing the cameras. "One boy was hit and died on the way to the hospital. Police are searching for any clues that could explain the motives in this senseless shooting or lead to the capture of the murderer."

"Why? Why my baby boy?" the broken man pleaded. "He didn't do anything to anyone! He was just riding his bike!"

The parents wept, and neighbors wrapped their arms around the couple to console them. The camera cut away to a school picture of a fresh-faced boy, grinning, a tooth missing, happy and apparently carefree. Innocence personified. Innocence lost.

Why do the innocent suffer?

Some of the most shocking images from the Holocaust are those of the children and elderly who were victims of that injustice. Their bodies shriveled yet living—if it could be called living. Working in the camps. Hiding. Dying. These helpless ones needed care, not mistreatment; shelter and protection, not punishment. They harmed no one and deserved to live full lives and die in dignity. But they didn't get that chance.

Why do the innocent suffer?

Native Americans, a proud but now subdued people, were driven from their homes by "newcomers" who claimed the land as their own. They were forced to march along what would come to be known as the Trail of Tears. Women and children stumbled, weeping, shivering in the frigid winter snows. Many died along the way. Decades earlier these same newcomers had raided another continent, carrying away its citizens to become slaves of their growing nation. Ironically, many of these newcomers believed they were allowed by God to engage in such barbarism.

Why do the innocent suffer?

How can God sit by and let evil affect the innocent, the gentle, the helpless souls who mean no harm to anyone? It's a fair question, put to a God who claims he represents all that is just: Why do the innocent suffer?

> If a plane crashes and 99 people die while one survives, it is called a miracle. Should the families of the 99 think so?
>
> —Judith Hayes, *In God We Trust: But Which One?*

OPEN FOR DISCUSSION

1. Share a personal example of a time when you or someone close to you experienced suffering for no just reason.

2. Do you agree with the following Bible passage, which teaches that evil people flourish and the innocent suffer? Give examples to support your answer.

> I envied the arrogant when I saw the prosperity of the wicked. They have no struggles; their bodies are healthy and strong. They are free from the burdens common to man; they are not plagued by human ills. . . . This is what the wicked are like—always carefree, they increase in wealth. Surely in vain have I kept my heart pure; in vain have I washed my hands in innocence. All day long I have been plagued; I have been punished every morning.
>
> —Psalm 73:3–5, 12–14

> Not long ago I was sleeping in a cabin in the woods and was awoken in the middle of the night by the sounds of a struggle between two animals. Cries of terror and extreme agony rent the night, intermingled with the sounds of jaws snapping bones and flesh being torn from limbs. One animal was being savagely attacked, killed and then devoured by another. A clearer case of a horrible event in nature, a natural evil, has never been presented to me. It seemed to me self-evident that the natural law that animals must savagely kill and devour each other in order to survive was an evil natural law and that the obtaining of this law was sufficient evidence that God did not exist.
>
> —Quentin Smith,
> *An Atheological Argument*
> *from Evil Natural Laws*

3. All suffering is the result of either an act of nature, an act (or lack thereof) of one or more beings (human or demonic), or a poor choice by the suffering individual. Many times it may be a combination of these. Which source(s) produced the suffering you described in question 1? Based on these categories, where do your feelings of blame or anger get directed? Explain.

4. When tornadoes, earthquakes, floods, disease, and other acts of nature cause tremendous suffering in the lives of people, which of the explanations listed below seem reasonable to you? Why?

_____ God is in control, and he orchestrates these hardships as a way to punish people or teach them lessons.

_____ God has given up control; therefore everything happens by chance.

_____ God is in control but still allows both good and bad things to happen.

_____ Acts of nature causing harm are really acts of the devil, not of God.

_____ All suffering caused by nature is the direct result of sin entering the world—sin that brought chaos within the system.

_____ No one knows the answer to such difficult questions—it's pointless to speculate.

> Believing God is the sovereign creator and in control of the world doesn't mean He is directly, causally connected with everything that happens on this earth. He doesn't make the decision to reach down and shake loose a rock to start every avalanche. When some people hear this kind of thinking, they get nervous. They think I'm limiting God. I'm not. But I am saying God doesn't ordinarily interfere with the natural course of the universe any more often than He directly interferes with man's choices.
>
> —Jay Kesler,
> _Making Life Make Sense_

5. If God isn't directly controlling everything that happens, what's a reasonable explanation for natural disasters?

6. Describe a time when you in some way caused or deserved the suffering you were experiencing. Did you still tend to want to blame someone or something other than yourself? Why?

7. Considering the pain we bring upon ourselves, why do you think God admonishes us in the Bible to "hate what is evil; cling to what is good" (Romans 12:9)?

STRAIGHT TALK

A Restraining Order

God has put at work in the world a restraining power that is buffering the effects of evil (2 Thessalonians 2:7). Were that restraint removed, we would have true hell on earth. In his book *The Goodness of God,* John Wenham adds, "Because sin deserves death and we are all sinners, it means that all our mercies are undeserved mercies. Any apparent unfairness in God's treatment of us arises not because some have too much punishment, but because some of us appear to have too little. None of us will ever receive harsher judgment than we ever deserve. . . . The marvel is, in the biblical view, not that men die for their sins, but that we remain alive in spite of them."

He [the Father in heaven] causes his sun to rise on the evil and the good, and sends rain on the righteous and the unrighteous.

—Matthew 5:45

8. In light of humankind's rejection of God and his ways, what point do you think C. S. Lewis is trying to get across when he states, "The question is not 'Why do the innocent suffer?' but rather 'Why don't we all suffer more?'" Do you agree with him? Why or why not?

STRAIGHT TALK

Beyond Words

We also rejoice in our sufferings, because we know that suffering produces perseverance; perseverance, character; and character, hope.

—Romans 5:3–4

Suffering is hard. And it can hurt at such a deep level. As we endure personal pain and suffering in our lives, we may often ask, "Why is this happening to me?" or complain, "Life isn't fair." But suffering is more than a cerebral problem. We are probably more intent on finding help and relief than on finding an explanation, and we certainly don't want someone giving us his or her idea of the "right answer" in an unfeeling way.

The Bible recognizes the need to go beyond explaining pain to a sufferer and so encourages us to "mourn with those who mourn" (Romans 12:15). It is a practice Jesus himself modeled. People going through dark valleys are looking for compassion, not just pat answers from someone more interested in being correct than in showing concern.

HEART OF THE MATTER

9. Can you think of any positive things that come out of our suffering? Share a personal example if you have one.

10. How do you suppose it's possible to love someone yet deny them something they really want (and you have the ability to provide)? Give examples.

> God whispers to us in our pleasures, speaks to us in our conscience, but shouts to us in our pains. Suffering is God's megaphone to rouse a deaf world.
>
> —C. S. Lewis

11. Has God ever used pain and suffering in your life to get your attention? What was he attempting to get across to you?

12. What possible alternatives to pain and suffering could God have used to capture your attention? Would they have been as effective?

STRAIGHT TALK

Comfort from God

As we encounter hard times, God offers words of encourage-ment and comfort. A few examples from the Bible are listed here.

He who did not spare his own Son, but gave him up for us all — how will he not also, along with him, graciously give us all things? . . . Who shall separate us from the love of Christ? Shall trouble or hardship or persecution or famine or nakedness or danger or sword? . . . No, in all these things we are more than conquerors through him who loved us. For I am convinced that neither death nor life, neither angels nor demons, neither the present nor the future, nor any powers, neither height nor depth, nor anything else in all creation, will be able to separate us from the love of God that is in Christ Jesus our Lord.

— Romans 8:32, 35, 37–39

Those who suffer according to God's will should commit themselves to their faithful Creator and continue to do good.

— 1 Peter 4:19

I consider that our present sufferings are not worth com-paring with the glory that will be revealed in us.

— Romans 8:18

We know that in all things God works for the good of those who love him, who have been called according to his purpose.

— Romans 8:28

13. People who refuse to let God into their lives have no promises in the Bible from him about finding any hope or benefits from suffering. However, the above verses assure those who do allow God leadership in their lives that something good can come from hard times. In what ways can the truth of these verses bring comfort in the suffering you endure?

14. Check the statement(s) below that best describes your position at this point. Share your selection with the rest of the group and give reasons for your response.

_____ I still cannot understand why God would allow innocent people to suffer.

_____ I can understand that suffering could be used to get someone's attention, but I think a loving God would think of a better way to make that happen.

_____ The benefits of God allowing people to make choices must far outweigh the costs.

_____ The suffering I have experienced in my own life has driven me away from God.

_____ It is good to know that suffering is only temporary.

_____ I don't understand it all, but I'm beginning to trust the way God is handling suffering in my life and in this world.

_____ Write your own brief phrase here: _____

_____

_____

Scripture for Further Study

- Job 1
- Job 13:15
- Job 38
- Matthew 19:26
- Luke 6:45
- John 9:1–12
- John 16:33

- Romans 5:3
- Romans 8:18
- Romans 12:12
- 1 Corinthians 10:13
- 2 Corinthians 4:17
- 2 Thessalonians 2:6–9
- James 1:2–18

Why Doesn't God Do Something?

A Good Story Gone Wrong?

The lead character in the spy novel you're reading is in a terrible fix. They've got him tied up and are planning to torch the cabin where he's hidden away. You lean forward in your chair as the action intensifies, wondering how he'll escape. The villains drench the foundation of the cabin in gasoline. With a single match, a bright yellow blaze envelops the walls in seconds.

The hero is trapped. He calls for help. He tries to loosen the cords that cut into his wrists. He kicks against the chair and tries to bash it against the wall and break free, but nothing works. Soon smoke billows into the room. He's overcome by the thick, dark clouds. He passes out. Within a few minutes his barely breathing form is engulfed in flames, and the hero is gone.

What? Dead? That can't be! You look to the next chapter, thinking he will have escaped somehow. Or maybe the cabin sequence was a dream. But the hero is dead. The bad guys have won. Evil triumphed. You hurl the book across the room.

"It's not fair! Why didn't the author write a better ending? Why did the good guy lose? That's not the way it should end!" But the author didn't write it that way. He allowed the hero to die.

That's how real life seems much of the time. When a little boy dies of leukemia in spite of hundreds of prayers, it seems as if the story isn't ending the right way. When the young woman with so much life ahead of her dies in a car accident, it's as if somebody made a huge mistake. When the relationship ends and you feel the crushing weight of failure and disappointment, you wish someone would rewrite your life's story.

After Elie Wiesel was a prisoner in a Nazi concentration camp at Birkenau, he described how a young boy was tortured and then hanged. The prisoners were forced to file by the boy, witnessing up close the punishment meted out on those who dared resist. The man behind Wiesel whispered through tears of rage, "Where is God now?" Wiesel later wrote, "In that moment, I heard a voice within me answer him, 'Where is he? Here he is—he is hanging here on this gallows.'" In the face of evil, God dies for many of us.

Is God out there writing the script or not? If God's in charge, why doesn't he get down here and write us a better ending?

OPEN FOR DISCUSSION

1. Have you ever wished that God would step in and rewrite the ending to a story in your life or the life of someone close to you? Share an example.

2. Habakkuk, an Old Testament prophet, cried out to God, "Your eyes are too pure to look on evil; you cannot tolerate wrong. Why then do you tolerate the treacherous? Why are you silent while the wicked swallow up those more righteous than themselves?" (Habakkuk 1:13). How do you think God would answer Habakkuk's accusations?

3. What does Habakkuk's ability to raise these issues with God (and their inclusion in the Bible) tell you about God's openness to tough questions directed at him?

> There is virtually nothing that the Christian will accept as evidence of God's evil. If disasters are compatible with the "goodness" of God, what could possibly qualify as contrary evidence? The "goodness" of God, it seems, is compatible with any state of affairs. While we evaluate a man with reference to his actions, we are not similarly permitted to judge God. God is immune from the judgment of evil as a matter of principle.
>
> —George Smith,
> *Atheism: The Case Against God*

4. Listed below is a set of scenarios describing how God could respond to the problem of suffering and evil. Select the one you like best and give some reasons for your selection. Which ones do you think are *not* good options?

- God could destroy us. He is supposedly all-powerful and perfectly capable of wiping out the human race. If there weren't any people, no one would hurt anyone and no one would get hurt. Nature could spew volcanic blasts, rattle the earth with quakes, and flood the plains, and the only life-forms affected would be plants and animals.

- God could handpick the evil people and eliminate them. All murderers, rapists, and terrorists—any truly wicked person—would go. Anyone who would eventually commit evil, even if it hadn't happened yet, would also be terminated. The rest of us would be left to live in peace.

- God could step in and override every evil act. When someone shoots another person, the guy who gets shot just gets up, grins, and goes on with life, like a character in a cartoon. If you drive off a cliff, you are a bit dazed for a minute or two, but then you shake it off. Our choices would make no difference. People would be immortal, like Superman, unable to get hurt or die.

- God could choose to stay out of things and let us fend for ourselves. We would just do our best and make our own choices and let the pieces fall where they may. He would watch—totally dispassionate, totally uninvolved, totally unconnected with our existence.

- God could periodically step in, unbeknownst to us. God could actually make a difference in minimizing evil or eliminating it at times. But we would never know what he was up to, and we would never know to whom he was going to show mercy or who was just out of luck.

- God could get a taste of what we go through, by experiencing the evil of the world personally and knowing what it feels like. We would then be able to see exactly how God would respond to the everyday frustrations and disappointments in facing evil and suffering firsthand.

5. Suppose God did step in and wipe out every trace of evil. In light of Romans 3:23 ("All have sinned and fall short of the glory of God"), what would that do to the human population? Where would that leave you?

6. If there were no sin (wrongdoing) in the world, do you think there would be any suffering and evil? Why or why not?

STRAIGHT TALK

Programmed to Love

Cliffe Knechtle has the following to say about love and choice.

> I deeply love my wife, Sharon. Suppose all I had to do to hear her say, "I love you, Cliffe" was to push a button in her back and out it would come. That wouldn't be love. That wouldn't be a relationship. It would be a programmed response from a computer. A relationship demands love. Love requires a choice. It cannot be forced. God created us in his image. That means when God commands, we can obey or disobey.

HEART OF THE MATTER

7. Given the above quote, why wouldn't it have been better if God had created us without an ability to choose evil in the first place?

8. Second Peter 3:9 reads, "The Lord is not slow in keeping his promise [to return to earth and put an end to evil], as some understand slowness. He is patient with you, not wanting anyone to perish, but everyone to come to repentance." What insight does this verse give concerning one reason why God currently tolerates evil?

9. What advantages are there in allowing people to see evil firsthand and then inviting them to reject it in favor of living under God's leadership? Do you believe this is the best way to deal with evil? Why or why not?

STRAIGHT TALK
The Ultimate Plan for Evil

Revelation 21:1, 3–5 describes God's ultimate plan for evil. In this passage the apostle John sees a vision of the future:

> I saw a new heaven and a new earth, for the first heaven and the first earth had passed away. . . . And I heard a loud voice . . . saying, "Now the dwelling of God is with men, and he will live with them. They will be his people, and God himself will be with them and be their God. He will wipe every tear from their eyes. There will be no more death or mourning or crying or pain, for the old order of things has passed away." He who was seated on the throne said, "I am making everything new!"

10. If you knew for sure that God would rid the world of evil somehow, in his own time, and bring about absolute justice, how would you feel about having to tolerate evil and suffering now?

STRAIGHT TALK

A Grand Finale

It seems that God allows evil so men and women who are separated from him can have an opportunity to turn back. If he eradicates all evil, he also stops the process by which people can come to him and eliminates the possibility of winning their hearts. People would no longer have their chance to know God and live in harmony with him for eternity.

God is just. He has a divine understanding of right and wrong. Not only can he hear each side's case, he also knows people's hidden motives and thoughts. As a result, when God promises justice, we can be sure that when it comes, it will be absolute and totally satisfying.

The story of God and humankind and evil isn't over. There's a grand finale yet to come, and it would be unfair to judge the "author" without letting him write the last chapter. The good news is, he already has the "rough draft" and it's found in the Bible — we know how the story is going to end. Some of the details will become clear only in the future, but based on what God has shown us already, we can trust him for a great ending.

In his book *Give Me an Answer,* Cliffe Knechtle recounts the following story.

> During World War II the guards at a Japanese prisoner-of-war camp would take the English soldiers out into the fields to do hard manual labor. At the end of one day the guards lined up the English prisoners and counted the tools. They found that one shovel was missing. A guard called out, "Who stole the shovel?" No one responded. The Japanese guard cocked his rifle and said, "All die! All die!"
>
> Suddenly one Scottish soldier stepped forward and said, "I stole the shovel." Instantly he was shot dead. His comrades gathered up his body and the remaining tools and went back to the prisoner-of-war compound. Back in the prison camp, the Japanese guards counted the tools again. They found that no shovel was missing. The Scottish soldier had sacrificed his life that his buddies might live.
>
> Two thousand years ago God became man. His name was Jesus Christ. He lived a perfect life. He never did anything wrong. He did not deserve to die. He stepped forward and bled and died on a cross to pay the penalty that you and I

deserve for having stolen, cheated, lied, dishonored our parents and ignored God. Your guilt and my guilt point to the wrong we have done. The cross of Jesus Christ points to the depth of God's love for us. You and I must decide to ask Christ for forgiveness and to commit our lives to him.

Referring to the story of Elie Wiesel in the concentration camp (see the introduction to this session), Philip Yancey observes, "The voice within Wiesel [which said God was hanging dead just like that boy] spoke truth: in a way, God did hang [there]. . . . God did not exempt even himself from human suffering. He too hung on a gallows, at Calvary, and that alone is what keeps me believing in a God of love."

---

11. What is your reaction to the claim that Jesus Christ, out of his great love for you, died on your behalf to pay the penalty for the evil in your life?

12. If Jesus Christ and his death for you were all God gave you to help you cope with evil in your life, would that be enough? What else would you need?

13. Check the statement(s) below that best describes your position at this point. Share your selection with the rest of the group and give reasons for your response.

_____ It makes no sense that God would allow evil in this world.

_____ It's impossible to really know why God does not do more to stop all this evil and suffering.

_____ I'm glad God has not wiped out all evil yet—otherwise I'd be gone, too.

_____ If God really loved us, he would not let us suffer so much.

_____ The benefits of God allowing us to make freewill choices far outweigh any costs.

_____ Write your own brief phrase here: _____

_____

_____

Scripture for Further Study

- Psalm 34:8
- Isaiah 43:2
- Isaiah 55:8
- Romans 5:8

- Romans 8:17–28
- James 1:2–12
- Hebrews 11
- Hebrews 12:12

Is the Devil for Real?

A Harmless Costume?

Mary winds her cart down the crowded aisles of the local Wal-Mart, shoving a handful of raisins at her wailing eighteen-month-old strapped in the front of the cart.

"Hurry up, Bobby," she calls to her lagging six-year-old son as they arrive at the aisle marked "Halloween costumes."

"There it is!" the boy exclaims as he races down the aisle, jumping over witches' wigs and little jars of green face paint that have been carelessly knocked to the floor. He snatches his choice off the rack and runs back to his weary mother, who is wiping his baby sister's nose.

"Here!" He shoves the costume in the cart. Mary looks down to see a plastic pitchfork and a red cape and horns coated with red glitter. Stapled to it is a plastic bag with the words "Devil makeup included." Mary picks up the costume. "Let's see what else we can find. . . . Maybe a nice cowboy outfit," she says firmly as she reaches to hang the devil outfit back on the rack.

"Mary?"

Mary turns to see her friend from the carpool. "Hi, Beth!"

"You look good in red," Beth says with a laugh.

Mary shakes her head. "I just can't bring myself to let Bobby run around in this thing. It seems so ... so, well, evil."

"Oh, what's the harm?" Beth says. "It's all just make-believe."

Mary quickly glances around at the shelves jammed with alternatives. She shrugs. "Yeah, I guess you're right. I mean, it's not like the devil is real or anything." She sighs as she tosses the devil outfit back into her cart.

He's called "Satan," "the devil," "the Dragon," and "the Serpent." Whether we picture him as a goofy guy with horns in red tights or as a dark, evil creature lurking about in a long, black cape, most of us have an image of Satan. But who hasn't dismissed that creature as a carryover from more superstitious times? Surely, in our scientific age, no one takes a personal, malevolent spiritual being seriously!

Is the devil real? Should he be feared? Or is he just a symbol, a myth, a personification of impersonal forces? This session will allow you to consider the reasons why we should take the matter of the devil seriously and explore what the Bible has to say about this fallen angel called Satan.

OPEN FOR DISCUSSION

1. Growing up, what did you believe about the devil? What most influenced your thinking?

2. Do you currently believe that an evil spiritual being exists? Why or why not? What is the value of trying to find out if such a being exists?

STRAIGHT TALK

Real Serious?

The search for the truth about the devil is not to prove there's evil in the universe; there is plenty of depravity bound up in the actions of people (see *People of the Lie* by M. Scott Peck) without having to refer to some spiritual force to prove that. Yet the Bible says evil extends beyond humans. No less an authority than Jesus himself believed in the existence of this fallen angelic being, and he warned others to take the devil seriously.

3. What difference does it make to you that Jesus believed in the devil? What other evidence for the devil's existence could be put forward?

STRAIGHT TALK

An Encounter with the Devil

The passage below tells of an encounter Jesus had with the devil just before Jesus started his public ministry.

Jesus was led by the Spirit into the desert to be tempted by the devil. After fasting forty days and forty nights, he was hungry. The tempter came to him and said, "If you are the Son of God, tell these stones to become bread."

Jesus answered, "It is written: 'Man does not live on bread alone, but on every word that comes from the mouth of God.'"

Then the devil took him to the holy city and had him stand on the highest point of the temple. "If you are the Son of God," he said, "throw yourself down. For it is written: 'He will command his angels concerning you, and they will lift you up in their hands, so that you will not strike your foot against a stone.'"

Jesus answered him, "It is also written: 'Do not put the Lord your God to the test.'"

Again, the devil took him to a very high mountain and showed him all the kingdoms of the world and their splendor. "All this I will give you," he said, "if you will bow down and worship me."

Jesus said to him, "Away from me, Satan! For it is written: 'Worship the Lord your God, and serve him only.'"

Then the devil left him, and angels came and attended him.

— Matthew 4:1–11

4. What did the devil seem to want from Jesus, and what tactics did he employ? How did Jesus get the devil to leave him alone?

5. The devil first shows up in the Bible in the Garden of Eden. As described in the following passage from Genesis, how does the devil try to get Eve to accept a distorted picture of God? Do you think Satan uses these same tactics today?

The serpent was more crafty than any of the wild animals the Lord God had made. He said to the woman, "Did God really say, 'You must not eat from any tree in the garden'?" The woman said to the serpent, "We may eat fruit from the trees in the garden, but God did say, 'You must not eat fruit from the tree that is in the middle of the garden, and you must not touch it, or you will die.'" "You will not surely die," the serpent said to the woman. "For God knows that when you eat of it your eyes will be opened, and you will be like God."

—Genesis 3:1–5

This crafty fallen angel knew exactly how to break down Adam and Eve's resistance. First, the devil called into question the accuracy of what God has said. By misquoting God's instructions, he planted a seed of doubt in Eve's mind. Second, he maligned God's character, questioning God's goodness and convincing Eve that God was keeping something beneficial from her. Finally, he promised that something wonderful would occur if she would simply take a bite. This final step painted a distorted picture of sinful actions, as if they contained only pleasure with no undesirable side effects. This is the same "one-two-three punch" that Satan often uses to break down people today.

—*The Journey: The Study Bible for Spiritual Seekers*, notes on Genesis

6. First Peter 5:8 says, "Your enemy the devil prowls around like a roaring lion looking for someone to devour." If the devil is an intelligent but rebellious angel, what do you think his motives are in trying to trip up people and gain additional "God rejecters" among humans?

7. In the early chapters of the book of Job, we find that Satan is allowed (within limits) to afflict Job through natural calamities and physical ailments. What role might Satan play in the evil and suffering experienced in our world today?

8. According to the verses below, what is the extent of the devil's power? What do you think about the fairness of this situation?

> We know that we [believers] are children of God, and that the whole world is under the control of the evil one.
>
> —1 John 5:19

> The god of this age [the devil] has blinded the minds of unbelievers, so that they cannot see the light of the gospel of the glory of Christ.
>
> —2 Corinthians 4:4

> Our struggle is not against flesh and blood, but against the rulers, against the authorities, against the powers of this dark world and against the spiritual forces of evil in the heavenly realms.
>
> —Ephesians 6:12

Satan himself masquerades as an angel of light.

—2 Corinthians 11:14

9. Why do you suppose God doesn't just eliminate Satan now?

HEART OF THE MATTER

10. What is your emotional response to the possibility of the devil's existence? What would help you determine, one way or the other, what the truth is concerning the devil?

11. Put into your own words the meaning behind what the Bible recommends in the following passages as defense against the devil.

> Submit yourselves, then, to God. Resist the devil, and he will flee from you.
> —James 4:7

> Be strong in the Lord and in his mighty power. Put on the full armor of God so that you can take your stand against the devil's schemes.
> —Ephesians 6:10–11

> God is faithful; he will not let you be tempted beyond what you can bear.
> —1 Corinthians 10:13

To me, as a Satanist, Satan represents the opposer to all Judeo-Christian ideals and ideology. Satan is the personification of Evil, where Evil means fleshly, unspiritual, and ungodly. Satan represents the fulfillment of the fleshly life, the enjoyment of the here and now, and the liberation of the psyche from the chains of Judeo-Christian guilt. . . .

Who is Satan? He is the mighty adversary of the inhuman death-cult religions. He is the light springing from the darkness of history. He is the true friend of mankind. But most of all . . . "The Prince of Darkness is a gentleman." (William Shakespeare, *King Lear*)

Hail Satan!

—Don David Scott

12. Check the statement(s) below that best describes your position at this point. Share your selection with the rest of the group and give reasons for your response.

_____ I still have no confidence that Satan exists.

_____ Satan may exist, but I don't think he plays an active role in my life or in the world around me.

_____ If God is all-powerful, I don't understand why he doesn't get rid of Satan now.

_____ This session left me with more questions than it answered.

_____ I believe Satan exists, and that frightens me.

_____ I believe Satan exists and is active in the world, but I am also confident that God is in control.

_____ I believe God can help me resist Satan, and I plan to ask for his help.

_____ I worry about the power Satan has to mess with my life.

_____ It bothers me that God has allowed Satan to have as much control as he has.

_____ Write your own brief phrase here: _____

_____

_____

Scripture for Further Study

- Genesis 3
- Matthew 4:1–11
- Matthew 13:19
- Mark 5:1–20
- Luke 10:17–20
- John 8:44
- John 10:10–18
- John 17:17

- 2 Corinthians 11:13–15
- Ephesians 2:2
- Ephesians 6:10–18
- 2 Thessalonians 2:1–12
- 1 John 3:7–10
- 1 John 4:4
- Revelation 20:7–10

How Could a Loving God Send People to Hell?

A Regular Guy

Richard's a decent fellow. At age sixty-eight, he's raised his family, paid his mortgage, celebrated the birth of five grandkids, and retired to a comfortable home in the country. He never did anything bad—unlike some people he knows. He never killed anyone, never pocketed company funds, never had an affair. He's just lived life. He hasn't bothered anyone, and everyone who knows him likes him.

Is this a man headed for hell?

"I figure, at the end of my life," Richard says, "if there's a God, he'll look at me and say, 'Now here's an average guy if I ever saw one. As long as you didn't do anything too terrible, come on in.' Frankly, I don't see how a loving God could send anyone to hell—let alone a regular guy like me."

Like Richard, many of us are counting on a points system of salvation, trusting that our good deeds will outweigh our bad. As long as God grades on a curve, most of us don't have a thing to worry about.

But what if the points don't add up in our favor? What if unkind intentions, selfish attitudes, lustful desires, and unseen motives factor in—all the things we thought were undetected? Worse, what if it's not enough just to tip the scales slightly in the direction of good? What if the presence of any sin is a problem?

But then again, some of us are hoping that God will just let all of us into heaven anyway.

"I've always heard God is love," Richard says. "Real love doesn't set up strict requirements for receiving it. It's unconditional. Certainly, limiting heaven only to people who follow Jesus is ridiculous. The whole idea of hell seems contrary to love."

Is Richard right? Will God give in and invite everyone into heaven after all?

Maybe there is no hell. Of course, it's a gamble to live as if hell doesn't exist, because if we're wrong, the result could be disastrous. But even if there is a hell, if we're there with most of our friends, it might not be so bad.

There is one definite way to find out. But do we really want to wait until it's too late to be certain? Can't we get our hands on any reliable information about the afterlife right now? So much is at stake. Even if there's only a five percent chance that hell exists, shouldn't we try to gain a reasonable certainty about where we're headed?

> Life can be beautiful, profound, and awe-inspiring, even without an irate god threatening us with eternal torment.
>
> —Judith Hayes, *In God We Trust: But Which One?*

OPEN FOR DISCUSSION

1. What is your position concerning the concept of hell? Choose from the statements below and give an explanation for your choice(s).

- No such place like hell exists.
- Hell is just a figurative idea without any reality attached to it.
- It doesn't really matter, because there's no such thing as an afterlife.
- Hell is total separation from God forever.
- Hell is present in the here and now.

- Hell is a fun place to party all the time.
- If people spend some time in hell, they will get to go to heaven later.
- Only the really, really wicked will go to hell.
- It doesn't really matter, because all people will go to heaven anyway.

2. On what basis have you come to your conclusions about hell? Which of the sources listed below strongly influence the position you take?

- spiritual books
- spiritual leaders
- popular opinion
- common sense
- the Bible
- religious upbringing
- hopeful thinking
- personal experience

3. How dependable are your sources of authority for your understanding about the idea of a hell? Use a scale from one to ten to indicate your response (one being a weak level of reliability and ten being a very strong level of reliability).

Some Say Yes, Some Say No

Opinions about the reality of hell — and the degrees of certainty regarding those opinions — range widely. Consider the following few examples.

I can hardly see how anyone ought to wish Christianity to be true: for if so the plain language of the text seems to show that the men who do not believe — and this would include my father, brother, and almost all of my best friends — will be everlastingly punished. And this is a damnable doctrine.

— Charles Darwin

Do not be afraid of those who kill the body but cannot kill the soul. Rather, be afraid of the One who can destroy both soul and body in hell.

— Matthew 10:28

The Lord Jesus, the Son of God, incarnate love himself, spoke more about the reality of hell and everlasting punishment for unbelievers than anyone else. Repeatedly, again and again in the discourses of Jesus, he warned his auditors, he pleaded with them to repent lest they perish.

— David L. Larsen

Now, if anything at all can be known to be wrong, it seems to me to be unshakably certain that it would be wrong to make any sentient being suffer eternally for any offense whatever.

— Antony Flew, *God, Freedom, and Immortality*

To rule by fettering the mind through fear of punishment in another world is just as base as to use force.

— Hypatia, Alexandrian mathematician, A.D. 415

4. On what basis do the people listed on the previous page believe or not believe that an actual place called hell exists? How does the reliability of their sources compare with the reliability of yours?

STRAIGHT TALK

Solemn Warnings

The Bible has much to say about hell:

> Enter through the narrow gate. For wide is the gate and broad is the road that leads to destruction, and many enter through it. But small is the gate and narrow the road that leads to life, and only a few find it.
>
> — Matthew 7:13–14

> If anyone's name was not found written in the book of life, he was thrown into the lake of fire.
>
> — Revelation 20:15

> The cowardly, the unbelieving, the vile, the murderers, the sexually immoral, those who practice magic arts, the idolaters and all liars — their place will be in the fiery lake of burning sulfur. This is the second death.
>
> — Revelation 21:8

> The Son of Man will send out his angels, and they will weed out of his kingdom everything that causes sin and all who do evil. They will throw them into the fiery furnace, where there will be weeping and gnashing of teeth.
>
> — Matthew 13:41–42 (see also Luke 16:19–31)

[Jesus said,] "Not everyone who says to me, 'Lord, Lord,' will enter the kingdom of heaven, but only he who does the will of my Father who is in heaven. Many will say to me on that day, 'Lord, Lord, did we not prophesy in your name, and in your name drive out demons and perform many miracles?' Then I will tell them plainly, 'I never knew you.'"

— Matthew 7:21–23

[Jesus said,] "O Jerusalem, Jerusalem, you who kill the prophets and stone those sent to you, how often I have longed to gather your children together, as a hen gathers her chicks under her wings, but you were not willing."

— Matthew 23:37

5. Based on the verses listed above, what are some of the reasons the Bible gives for why people end up in hell?

6. Based on the verses listed above, what observations can you make about what hell is really like?

7. What do you think of the following objections to the idea of hell? Can you come up with some of your own?

- If God is just, sending people to hell would be unfair.

- If God is love, hell would not be a result of unconditional love.
- Hell as a punishment for sin doesn't fit the crime.
- "Good" people—though admittedly not perfect—ought to be rewarded for their goodness, not punished for their mistakes.

[The Bible] goes on about the wailing and gnashing of teeth. It comes in one verse after another, and it is quite manifest to the reader that there is a certain pleasure in contemplating the wailing and gnashing of teeth, or else it would not occur so often.

—Bertrand Russell

STRAIGHT TALK

God's Outlook on Hell

Ultimately, God doesn't send anyone to hell; people choose to go there. People reject God in a variety of ways and then spend an eternity living with the very choices they've made while here on earth. If they invite God to forgive their sins through Christ, to be involved in their lives, to lead and direct them, to be Lord over all their decisions, then heaven is the place where that continues, only more so. If, on the other hand, people avoid God, find his laws restrictive and objectionable, prefer he not interfere in their plans, and reject his overtures of reconciliation, then hell is the place where that way of living is allowed forever. C. S. Lewis pointed this out very well when he said, "There are two kinds of people in the world: those who say to God, 'Your will be done' and those to whom God says, 'Your will be done.'"

The Bible emphasizes God's attitude toward people heading for hell:

> "As surely as I live, declares the Sovereign Lord, I take no pleasure in the death of the wicked, but rather that they turn from their ways and live. Turn! Turn from your evil ways! Why will you die, O house of Israel?"
>
> — Ezekiel 33:11

> He is patient with you, not wanting anyone to perish, but everyone to come to repentance.
>
> — 2 Peter 3:9

DISCUSSION FIVE
63

8. What is your reaction to the assertions listed on the previous page? Which ideas do you agree with and which do you disagree with? What conclusions can be drawn about God's desire concerning everyone's eternal destiny?

HEART OF THE MATTER

God is not merely a doddering old grandfather with a white beard who sits on a throne in the sky and smiles as he lets everyone pass by. He's not hanging around saying, "Well, Hitler, you murdered a few folks at Dachau, Buchenwald and Auschwitz, but I understand you're simply a product of your environment. I'm all-forgiving; enter heaven." That's not being loving—that's amoral. Instead of asking, "How could a caring God allow a hell to exist?" the question ought to be, "How could a caring God not allow a hell to exist?"

—Cliffe Knechtle, *Give Me an Answer*

9. Hell can be described as the place where God finally confines sin and evil—where he puts boundaries around it once and for all so it doesn't pollute the rest of the universe. How do you feel about the hope that evil will not last forever?

10. Do you think that when people avoid or reject God and his involvement in their lives, they realize they are actually choosing hell? On a more personal level, have *you* resisted God at times in your life? Explain.

Justice and Love for All

In his book *Give Me an Answer,* Cliffe Knechtle tells the following story:

> Two close friends graduated from college in Australia. One became a judge and the other a banker. One day the banker was arrested for embezzlement of one million dollars. He was to be tried before his friend. The courtroom was packed. The jury deliberated. They delivered the verdict — guilty. The judge then gave the sentence. He leveled the harshest fine possible against his friend. The crowd gasped in amazement. But then everyone watched in wonder as the judge stood, took off his robe, walked around the bar and extended his hand to his friend. He said, "I have sold my house, taken all my savings out of my account. I have paid the fine I just leveled against you." That is how it works with Christ's death on the cross. In one act both justice and love are found. And it's free for all to receive.

We must picture Hell as a state where everyone is perpetually concerned about his own dignity and advancement, where everyone has a grievance, and where everyone lives the deadly serious passions of envy, self-importance, and resentment.

—C. S. Lewis

11. Can hell, God's justice, and God's love all be real and true at the same time? Explain.

If every Christian could spend one minute in the fires of hell, he would become a soul winner the rest of his life and seek to warn men and women of the terrible and tragic fate that awaits those who believe not the gospel.

—General Booth, Founder, Salvation Army

CHARTING YOUR JOURNEY

12. Check the statement(s) below that best describes your position at this point. Share your selection with the rest of the group and give reasons for your response.

_____ I see no reason to believe that a place called hell exists.

_____ Maybe hell exists, but it can't really be forever.

_____ I am still unsure how I feel about hell.

_____ The idea of hell bothers me because I am unsure if I will end up there or not.

_____ I am unable to reconcile the thought of a loving God condemning someone to hell.

_____ I believe that hell exists, and I am grateful that God has given us a way out.

_____ I believe that hell as described in the Bible exists, but I'm pretty sure I'm not going there.

_____ The worst thing about hell would be separation from God.

_____ I don't think hell is anything to worry about.

_____ It bothers me that some of my friends and family may wind up in hell.

_____ Write your own brief phrase here: _____

_____

_____

Scripture for Further Study

- Genesis 3
- Deuteronomy 30:11–19
- Proverbs 14:12
- Isaiah 53:6
- Ezekiel 33:1–20
- Matthew 7:7–14, 21–29
- Matthew 16:21–28
- Matthew 18:23–35
- Matthew 19:16–30
- Matthew 25:31–46
- Luke 16:19–31
- John 3:16
- Romans 1–3
- Romans 6:23
- 1 Corinthians 1:18–19
- 1 Corinthians 2:9
- 2 Thessalonians 2:9–10
- 1 Peter 3:18
- 2 Peter 3:1–13
- Revelation 20:10

Is There Really a Heaven?

Beyond the Pale?

How can we be sure there is some kind of existence beyond death? Is there evidence we can trust? It seems lots of people want to be in heaven only because they don't want to risk hell. If all the less than legitimate thrills of life are taken away, is the result a fleecy, feather-filled forever?

The way it's portrayed in the popular mind-set, heaven appears to be a bland, banal place—a sea of harp players dressed in white robes, choirs of angels singing incessantly. If this sort of sanitized setting is our eternal home, most of us wonder which would be worse: a painless, boring heaven or a painful but interesting hell.

Maybe all this life-after-death stuff is a myth—like the Easter Bunny and nursery rhymes. We tell our children stories about heaven, but we know we really don't have any solid basis for such fables. Maybe when we die, we die, and that's it. Or if there is an afterlife, it won't be at all like what we've imagined. Besides, if we all have such differing concepts of what a great forever would look like, how can heaven hope to meet all our varied expectations? Can we even know what it will be like?

So often people point to rewards in the afterlife as if heaven makes up for all we've had to endure here on earth. Isn't that just a way to cope? And does

> To believe that consciousness can survive the wreck of the brain is like believing that 70 mph can survive the wreck of the car.
>
> —Frank Zindler

heaven really get God off the hook for all the pain that's happened down here? It sounds as if heaven was invented to help people justify life's frustrations and God's failures. If we put all our hope in something that can't be seen, we're betting everything—*everything*—on a long shot. That just doesn't make sense.

In this session we will explore reasons for believing in an afterlife and get a clearer picture of why the Bible teaches that heaven is real and thrilling.

OPEN FOR DISCUSSION

1. Do you believe there is some kind of life after death? What reasons do you have for your answer?

2. Which of the following options do you believe happens after death? What influenced your thinking?

- nothing
- heaven
- hell
- reincarnation
- nirvana
- other: _____

3. Which of the concerns or questions listed below have you had as you've thought about heaven?

- Will it be boring?
- Is it just wishful thinking—does it even exist?
- Will we be able to recognize people?
- Will it be sad if every loved one isn't there?
- Will we become angels with halos and wings?
- Isn't eternity a long time to be at the same place?
- Other concerns: _____

4. When Jesus talked about heaven to his disciples, he said, "In my Father's house are many rooms; if it were not so, I would have told you. I am going there to prepare a place for you. And if I go and prepare a place for you, I will come back and take you to be with me that you also may be where I am" (John 14:2–3). What do the phrases "many rooms" and "prepare a place" convey to you about the personal touches and loving concern Jesus says await you in heaven? How might this teaching address fears about heaven being boring?

5. Some people believe that heaven is the place for those who do good and hell is the place for those who do bad. If we have to be good to enter heaven, how good do we have to be? Can anyone know for sure if he or she has been good enough?

6. According to your understanding of the Bible, on what basis do sinful people gain entrance into heaven? Do you believe people can be confident that they're going to heaven? Why or why not?

HEART OF THE MATTER

7. How confident are you that you will spend eternity in heaven? What is the basis for your level of confidence?

8. What difference does it make to have assurance now about where you'll spend eternity?

STRAIGHT TALK

Take Heart

If heaven is the place where there is no pain and suffering, what are we to make of our hardships now? What is God's attitude toward our plight? Consider these insights:

> The Bible never belittles disappointment . . . but it does add one key word: temporary.
>
> — Philip Yancey, *Disappointment with God*

> [Jesus said,] "I have told you these things, so that in me you may have peace. In this world you will have trouble. But take heart! I have overcome the world."
>
> — John 16:33

> Where is God when it hurts? He is in *you,* the one hurting, not in *it,* the thing that hurts.
>
> — Dr. Paul Brand and Philip Yancey,
> *Pain: The Gift Nobody Wants*

9. Although God doesn't promise you freedom from pain in this life, is it enough that he offers to be with you now and care for you forever in a place totally void of evil and suffering, called heaven? Why or why not?

This is the testimony: God has given us eternal life, and this life is in his Son. He who has the Son has life; he who does not have the Son of God does not have life. I write these things to you who believe in the name of the Son of God so that you may know that you have eternal life.

—1 John 5:11–13

The city does not need the sun or the moon to shine on it, for the glory of God gives it light. . . . The nations will walk by its light. . . . Nothing impure will ever enter it, nor will anyone who does what is shameful or deceitful, but only those whose names are written in the Lamb's book of life.

—Revelation 21:23–24, 27

10. At this point in your spiritual journey, how important is the concept of heaven to you?

11. Check the statement(s) below that best describes your position at this point. Share your selection with the rest of the group and give reasons for your response.

_____ I believe that when we die, that's it—it is all over.

_____ Even if there is a heaven, it can't be that great.

_____ I have a lot of confidence that I will go to heaven when I die.

_____ Eternity in heaven won't compensate for life's troubles.

_____ I am confident that heaven exists, but I'm unsure if I'll end up there.

_____ I am fairly certain I will wind up in heaven when I die.

_____ I believe that most everyone will go to heaven.

_____ Write your own brief phrase here: _____

_____

_____

Scripture for Further Study

- Genesis 2:1–7
- Psalm 14:1–3
- Isaiah 6:1–7
- Isaiah 66:1–2
- Matthew 6:19–21
- Matthew 8:5–13
- John 1:10–13
- John 14:1–6

- Acts 1:1–11
- Romans 6:23
- Romans 10:9
- Philippians 3:12–21
- 1 Peter 3:18
- 1 John 1
- Revelation 3:20–22

Recommended Resources

Ken Boa and Larry Moody, *I'm Glad You Asked* (Chariot Victor, 1995).

Gregory Boyd and Edward Boyd, *Letters from a Skeptic* (Chariot Victor, 1994).

Paul Brand and Philip Yancey, *The Gift of Pain* (Zondervan, 1997).

C. Stephen Evans, *Why Believe?* (Eerdmans, 1996).

David Hewetson and David Miller, *Christianity Made Simple* (InterVarsity, 1983).

Cliffe Knechtle, *Give Me an Answer* (InterVarsity, 1986).

Cliffe Knechtle, *Help Me Believe* (InterVarsity, 2000).

Andrew Knowles, *Finding Faith* (Lion, 1994).

Peter Kreeft and Ronald Tacelli, *Handbook of Christian Apologetics* (InterVarsity, 1994).

C. S. Lewis, *A Grief Observed* (HarperSanFransisco, 2001).

C. S. Lewis, *Mere Christianity* (HarperSanFransisco, 2001).

C. S. Lewis, *Miracles* (HarperSanFransisco, 2001).

C. S. Lewis, *The Screwtape Letters* (HarperSanFransisco, 2001).

Paul Little, *Know What You Believe* (Chariot Victor, 1987).

Paul Little, *Know Why You Believe* (InterVarsity, 2000).

Lee Strobel, *The Case for Christ* (Zondervan, 1998).

Lee Strobel, *The Case for Faith* (Zondervan, 2000).

Philip Yancey, *Disappointment with God* (Zondervan, 1997).

Philip Yancey, *Where Is God When It Hurts?* (Zondervan, 1997).

Willow Creek Association
Vision, Training, Resources for Prevailing Churches

This resource was created to serve you and to help you in building a local church that prevails! Since 1992, the Willow Creek Association (WCA) has been linking like-minded, action-oriented churches with each other and with strategic vision, training, and resources. Now a worldwide network of over 6,400 churches from more than ninety denominations, the WCA works to equip Member Churches and others with the tools needed to build prevailing churches. Our desire is to inspire, equip, and encourage Christian leaders to build biblically functioning churches that reach increasing numbers of unchurched people, not just with innovations from Willow Creek Community Church in South Barrington, Illinois, but from any church in the world that has experienced God-given breakthroughs.

WILLOW CREEK CONFERENCES
Each year, thousands of local church leaders, staff and volunteers—from WCA Member Churches and others—attend one of our conferences or training events. Conferences offered on the Willow Creek campus in South Barrington, Illinois, include:

Prevailing Church Conference: Foundational training for staff and volunteers working to build a prevailing local church.

Prevailing Church Workshops: More than fifty strategic, day-long workshops covering seven topic areas that represent key characteristics of a prevailing church; offered twice each year.

Promiseland Conference: Children's ministries; infant through fifth grade.

Student Ministries Conference: Junior and senior high ministries.

Willow Creek Arts Conference: Vision and training for Christian artists using their gifts in the ministries of local churches.

Leadership Summit: Envisioning and equipping Christians with leadership gifts and responsibilities; broadcast live via satellite to eighteen cities across North America.

Contagious Evangelism Conference: Encouragement and training for churches and church leaders who want to be strategic in reaching lost people for Christ.

Small Groups Conference: Exploring how developing a church *of* small groups can play a vital role in developing authentic Christian community that leads to spiritual transformation.

To find out more about WCA conferences, visit our website at www.willowcreek.com.

PREVAILING CHURCH REGIONAL WORKSHOPS
Each year the WCA team leads several, two-day training events in select cities across the United States. Some twenty day-long workshops are offered in topic areas including leadership, next-

generation ministries, small groups, arts and worship, evangelism, spiritual gifts, financial stewardship, and spiritual formation. These events make quality training more accessible and affordable to larger groups of staff and volunteers.

To find out more about Prevailing Church Regional Workshops, visit our website at www.willowcreek.com.

WILLOW CREEK RESOURCES™

Churches can look to Willow Creek Resources™ for a trusted channel of ministry tools in areas of leadership, evangelism, spiritual gifts, small groups, drama, contemporary music, financial stewardship, spiritual transformation, and more. For ordering information, call (800) 570-9812 or visit our website at www.willowcreek.com.

WCA MEMBERSHIP

Membership in the Willow Creek Association as well as attendance at WCA Conferences is for churches, ministries, and leaders who hold to a historic, orthodox understanding of biblical Christianity. The annual church membership fee of $249 provides substantial discounts for your entire team on all conferences and Willow Creek Resources, networking opportunities with other outreach-oriented churches, a bimonthly newsletter, a subscription to the *Defining Moments* monthly audio journal for leaders, and more.

To find out more about WCA membership, visit our website at www.willowcreek.com.

WILLOWNET (WWW.WILLOWCREEK.COM)

This Internet resource service provides access to hundreds of Willow Creek messages, drama scripts, songs, videos, and multimedia ideas. The system allows you to sort through these elements and download them for a fee.

Our website also provides detailed information on the Willow Creek Association, Willow Creek Community Church, WCA membership, conferences, training events, resources, and more.

WILLOWCHARTS.COM (WWW.WILLOWCHARTS.COM)

Designed for local church worship leaders and musicians, WillowCharts.com provides online access to hundreds of music charts and chart components, including choir, orchestral, and horn sections, as well as rehearsal tracks and video streaming of Willow Creek Community Church performances.

THE NET (HTTP://STUDENTMINISTRY.WILLOWCREEK.COM)

The NET is an online training and resource center designed by and for student ministry leaders. It provides an inside look at the structure, vision, and mission of prevailing student ministries from around the world. The NET gives leaders access to complete programming elements, including message outlines, dramas, small group questions, and more. An indispensable resource and networking tool for prevailing student ministry leaders!

CONTACT THE WILLOW CREEK ASSOCIATION

If you have comments or questions, or would like to find out more about WCA events or resources, please contact us:

Willow Creek Association
P.O. Box 3188, Barrington, IL 60011-3188
Phone: (800) 570-9812 or (847) 765-0070
Fax: (888) 922-0035 or (847) 765-5046
Web: www.willowcreek.com

TOUGH QUESTIONS

Garry Poole and Judson Poling

"The profound insights and candor captured in these guides will sharpen your mind, soften your heart, and inspire you and the members of your group to find vital answers together."   —Bill Hybels

This second edition of Tough Questions, designed for use in any small group setting, is ideal for use in seeker small groups. Based on more than five years of field-tested feedback, extensive revisions make this best-selling series easier to use and more appealing than ever for both participants and group leaders.

Softcover

How Does Anyone Know God Exists?	ISBN 0-310-24502-8
What Difference Does Jesus Make?	ISBN 0-310-24503-6
How Reliable Is the Bible?	ISBN 0-310-24504-4
How Could God Allow Suffering and Evil?	ISBN 0-310-24505-2
Don't All Religions Lead to God?	ISBN 0-310-24506-0
Do Science and the Bible Conflict?	ISBN 0-310-24507-9
Why Become a Christian?	ISBN 0-310-24508-7
Leader's Guide	ISBN 0-310-24509-5

Pick up a copy at your favorite local bookstore today!

GRAND RAPIDS, MICHIGAN 49530 USA

WWW.ZONDERVAN.COM

THE COMPLETE BOOK OF QUESTIONS

Garry Poole

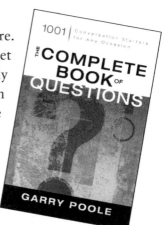

Everyone has a story to tell or an opinion to share. *The Complete Book of Questions* helps you get the conversational ball rolling. Created especially for seeker small groups, these questions can jumpstart any conversation. They invite people to open up about themselves and divulge their thoughts, and provide the spark for stimulating discussions. This generous compilation of questions can be used in just about any context to launch great conversations.

Questions cover ten thematic categories, from light and easy questions such as "What room in your house best reflects your personality?" to deeper, more spiritual questions such as, "If God decided to visit the planet right now, what do you think he would do?" *The Complete Book of Questions* is a resource that can help small group leaders draw participants out and couples, friends, and families get to know one another better.

Softcover: ISBN 0-310-24420-X

Pick up a copy at your favorite local bookstore today!

GRAND RAPIDS, MICHIGAN 49530 USA
WWW.ZONDERVAN.COM

THE THREE HABITS OF HIGHLY CONTAGIOUS CHRISTIANS

Garry Poole

A small group discussion guide that will ignite the heart to reach seekers for Christ.

Living an intentionally contagious Christian life really matters! It's worth the effort and risks involved. *The Three Habits of Highly Contagious Christians* will help you reach out to seekers naturally by

1. building relationships
2. sharing a verbal witness
3. inviting people to outreach events

Discover how to cultivate authentic relationships with seekers, not as projects to work on but as friends and companions with common interests. You'll learn practical ways to build bridges of trust while checking yourself for the underlying attitudes that drive seekers away. From being on the lookout for windows of opportunity to talk with seekers about Christ, to bringing them to a church service or outreach, this study helps you find ways to bring people to Christ easily and naturally.

Each session begins with a thought-provoking story, then uses questions that generate honest, open group discussion. Exercises encourage participants to apply principles to their own lives. *The Three Habits of Highly Contagious Christians* challenges believers to individually commit to specific choices that could make all the difference in the lives of seeking friends and family members.

Softcover: ISBN 0-310-24496-X

Pick up a copy at your favorite local bookstore today!

GRAND RAPIDS, MICHIGAN 49530 USA
WWW.ZONDERVAN.COM